God's Words,
My Healing

God's Words, My Healing

Terri Johnson

BookLocker
St. Petersburg, Florida

Published by BookLocker.com, Inc., St. Petersburg, Florida.

Printed on acid-free paper.

BookLocker.com, Inc.

2019

Library of Congress Cataloging in Publication Data
Johnson, Terri
God's Words, My Healing
Healing/General, Body, Mind, Spirit | Angel's & Spirit Guides, Body,
Mind, Spirit | Healing/Prayer & Spiritual, Body, Mind, Spirit
Library of Congress Control Number: 2019912306

Dedication

In loving memory of
Jarvis (Hot Water) Johnson
My brother and dear friend
Jerry Carroll Johnson
July 5, 1961 — March 15-2007

This book is dedicated to my parents, Jerry and Carolyn Johnson, my brother, Troy Johnson, my sister, Tressa Johnson Harn, and especially, to my late brother, Jerry Carroll Johnson. He was a coal miner, a father, a son, a hunter, an uncle, and so much more.

After my brother passed away on March 15, 2007, I got sick. After six months of taking pills, and sleeping at the graveyard, I started writing, and the writing ended up, being what I needed to heal myself. Through God's words, I am healed.

May He heal you, as He has healed me. These words are my sufferings, my joy, my sadness, my trials, and my tribulation. I have fought all kinds of evil spirits, just as so many others among us fight spiritual warfare. It is not a battle against flesh and blood. It is a war of the spirit. The act of writing these devotional poems down has healed me. These are God's words, and they are my healing.

God bless you all who read this book!

Table of Contents

God's Words,
My Healing

Traveling in the Spirit

Hello. It's just me.
You thought I had gone, but
I will never leave you.
I must carry on.

I have work to do,
even though I can't be seen.
If you would *just* listen,
a sign to you I'll bring.

I'm traveling in spirit, and
my spirit is all around, even
when you can't see me,
I can still be found.

I loved you
more than anything.
Know that I am right beside you,
and happiness I will still bring.

I will never leave you,
for I am deep in your heart.
I have always loved you,
and we will never part.

– *Jarvis*

Crown of Thorns

I can't believe they put a crown of thorns on your head.
The blood ran down, and they all thought you were dead.
When you said, "it is finished," they all thought it was done;
they just didn't realize that you were God's son.

Satan was deceived that very day.
A king on the cross they did slay.
They made you carry your own cross.
It must have been that they were all lost.

If Satan had known,
he would have told them to let you down,
and we would be lost—no salvation ever found.

So, thank you Lord for that day at Calvary
when you died on the cross to set us all free.

So, choose today, and please don't wait,
for when Jesus comes back,
It will be too late.

If I Could Have Just One More

If I could have just one more day,
I know just what I'd do and just what I'd say.

I'd come down to your room
and walk through the door,
get up on the bed,
roll you over,
and get back on the floor.

I'd ask you if you're going to be okay,
if I could help in any way.
Then I'd fix your pillows,
and we'd start our day.

Then I'd turn to you,
and this is what I'd say:
"My dearest brother, I love you,
and I have missed you every day.

"You're so special to me,
and I love you so much.
I really love your smile,
and your hand I used to touch."

We'd watch *Dumb and Dumber*
and, *O Brother, Where Art Thou?* too.

We'd watch old westerns
and laugh like we used to do.

Then I'd thank you for always encouraging me,
and I would never leave your room,
because if we only had one more day,
you'd be leaving soon.

I'd say, "I wish you could stay, and never ever go.
I miss, and I love you, brother. This you surely know."
I'd pick up the remote, and we'd channel surf,
find a good western, one of the kind you liked the most.

Then I'd get on my knees and beg God to heal you
and let you get out of bed and walk,
and we'd be on our way
to spend just one more day.

My Brother in the Mirror

I looked in the mirror,
and to my surprise,
I saw my brother
standing by my side.

I turned around to look,
and then you were gone.
This is when I felt
that I was all alone.

Then I heard a voice,
and this is what it seemed to say:
"I was passing by your house,
but I must be on my way.

"I have so many to visit;
I'm a very busy man.
Being in the spirit,
Humans just don't understand.

"I'll come back often
just to see you, though.
Remember what you saw in the mirror
was me standing there beside you.

"Thank you, sister,
for helping me each day.
Now I have to go.
I must be on my way."

My Father, My Friend

Dear Father, I love you.
You're so special to me.
No matter what I've done,
you've always set me free.

I've loved you from the start,
and I will love you 'til the end.
No matter what I've done,
you have always been my friend.

You died upon the cross
on that awful day, but you've
reached right down and touched me
in a very special way.

I'm waiting for the day
when you will come again.
No matter what I've done,
you've always been my friend.

I love you, my dear Father.
Thanks again for all you've done.
If it weren't for you, dear Father,
I'd still be on the run.

You reached right down and touched me
on that special day.
Thank you, Lord, for every little thing
you've ever done for me.

Now I'm on my way, and
I can't wait to see you. I'll hold on
tight to you up until the end.
Thank you for always being my friend

To My Son

No more pills, no more tears,
no more sad times, and no more fears.
No more night — only day.
This is where I long to stay.

The streets are pure, transparent gold,
the gates studded with precious stones.
We all belong right here,
splendor to behold.

Remember me, I'm always around,
even though my mortal flesh can't be found.
You can't touch, or see me, and that is okay;
I'll still be near you every step of the way.

You can't see me, but I'll send you a sign.
Son, we always used to have the best of times.
So, listen to the ducks, and the funny sounds they make.
It probably will be me, make no mistake.

I sent angels from Heaven to watch over you,
And guess what, son? Now I'm an angel too!
Know when you see those things we loved, I'm there.
It's me, your dad, sending you all of my love

— Jarvis

Never Over Mine

Oh, my goodness! It's me.
You thought that I had left.
You thought I'd gone away
and left you by yourself.

Well, I didn't really leave.
I can't believe you thought I would.
I will never leave you, and
This you should have known.

When you think of me,
remember that I always cared.
Shut your eyes and think of me,
and I will be right there.

Always know I love you dearly.
You were all so very kind.
I would never have chosen another family.
Never. You're all mine

So, know how much I love you.
Know I am always near.
Look right down inside your heart.
Hear my voice in there.

Know that I go with you everywhere you go.
I will never leave you. This, I hope you know.

The Day Before Thanksgiving

Brother, it's the day before Thanksgiving,
and you're nowhere around.
I went down into your room,
but you just can't be found.

Right now, I'm really missing you.
You were such a light,
and when a smile spread across your face,
the light was just so bright.

Our Thanksgiving Day will never be the same.
I sit here now, and blame your wife
for everything you and your son suffered,
every bit of strife. Then we all forgave her.

Our Thanksgiving Day, will never be
the same without you. What is done is done.
So, I guess it's goodbye for now,
my Dear Brother, I wish you hadn't gone.

Happy Thanksgiving Day to you,
special, special you.
We all feel lost without you,
and we always will love you, too.

Brother Where Are You?

Brother, I sure do miss you.
I don't know what to say,
but I sure have missed you,
since you went away.

Today makes eight months
to the day, since you left me,
and Brother I sure do miss you.
I hope you still can see.

Brother, I sure have missed you,
and my days are full of tears,
but since that day, I've found Jesus,
and now I have no more fear.

I'm not afraid to die because
I know you wait for me.
Jesus is now my comfort.
Thank God he set me free

"Sister, I'm up in heaven,
above the sky so blue.
When you feel sad, and lonely
it makes me sad, and lonely too.

"Hey there sister, when you feel blue,
just remember what I say,
blue don't look good on you!"

Looking Down from Heaven

Looking down from heaven,
I thought I heard you say,
"Lord, why did you take him?
Why did you take him away?"

That is when I knew
you didn't understand.
I've been waiting for him to come
and take me to the Promise Land.

The morning when I left, I didn't go alone.
The Lord came and got me. He took me by the hand.
He stood there with his Angels, right on either side.
He said, "Come on with me, I'll be your heavenly guide."

I said, "Okay, Lord, take me on away.
In Heaven with you is where I want to stay."
I hurt no more, no pain for me, for the Lord
came and got me, and he set me free.

— *Jarvis*

I Really Miss You

I really miss you,
And I wish you didn't have to go.
I love you so much,
this I hope you know.

I'm waiting for the day
when I can see your face again
Not only were you my brother,
You were a *good* brother to the end.

Things in this life
are never what they seem
I'm holding onto my faith
and to all of my dreams.

I wish that I could touch you —
see your beautiful face.
You were the most beautiful man
ever to live in this place.

There's not another like you.
No, no one anywhere.
I wish that I could run my hands
Through your long, dark, curly hair.

Just to see, and touch you,
if only one more time,
Brother, I love you dearly,
you, a man that was so fine.

Home in Heaven

I made it home to Heaven
where I so longed to be.
I have nothing left down here
except my son, and family.

Hold on to the Lord
with all of your might,
and one night when you least expect it,
you too will take that Heavenly flight.

Come up here to be with Jesus,
I'll be waiting right here for you,
up above the clouds where
the sky is always blue.

The only way to get here
is to let the sweet Lord in,
and once you get to Heaven,
Your journey's over, friend.

I'm Saving You a Place

I'm up here in Heaven,
and I'm waiting here for you.
I just can't figure out
why you are so blue.

I made it home to Heaven,
and there is nowhere I'd rather be.
I'm in the most beautiful place
someday you'll get to see.

It is such a wonderful place,
I can't wait to see you again.
Not only were you my sister,
you were also my dearest friend.

I'm saving you a place
right beside of me.
When you too get to Heaven,
free you'll also be.

Don't you shed a tear,
and don't you cry for me.
The day I left was sad for you,
but it wasn't supposed to be.

I'm truly sorry that I left you,
but please don't feel sad, and blue,
'cause when your job on earth is done,
he'll come and get you too.

When I Woke Up Today

When I woke up today,
I was somewhere new.
People everywhere,
but no one looked like you.

I got up, and turned around —
opened up my eyes.
All my family that was gone
was standing by my side.
That is when I knew.

There were people I hadn't seen in years,
and I noticed all the love.
No more tears fell anywhere,

and I saw a great white light
shining all the way through
a figure who didn't speak,
and that is when I knew

I'd made it home to Heaven,
where everyone longs to be.
If you change your life,
you can come and be with me.

— Jarvis

Hello!

Hello!
Good morning!
When I passed by,
and looked at you,
a tear was in your eye.

Please don't be so sad,
and please don't even cry.
I'll come around and visit
when you close your eyes.

When you think of me,
I'll be right here close by.
I have a pair of shiny wings,
and now I get to fly!

I come sometimes; sometimes I go.
I'm always near, you know.
When times get hard, I'll see
you through each and every blow.

So, here I am with Jesus,
walking by his side. I'm happy now,
but don't forget,
You'll always be my pal.

At Calvary

The blood ran down your face.
They all thought you were dead.
They'd placed a crown of thorns upon your head.

They beat and hurt you,
and that's a thing they'll never forget,
because in the end,
you had no regret.

You let them kill you,
saying nothing through the day.
You let them crucify you.
You let them have their way.

When you said "It's finished,"
it had just begun.
You are our precious Savior,
God's only begotten son.

Thank you, my dear Lord,
for what you did for me.
You died at Calvary,
and set me free.

He Comes to Visit

I saw him standing in the room.
He said, "I'll be back soon."
He went to a place in the sky,
but he comes to visit you, and I.

He said, Miss Loria, to tell you
he will be back by to see you soon.
He'll be coming by,
And when he comes, you'll know why.

Jarvis, he comes and goes.
He said he loves you, Laura.
He'll be back in a couple of hours.

He will stoop down.
His feet will touch the ground.
I better not fly too low.
You know how that could go.

So, girl, he will be by to see you.
He loves to visit you.
A table is set for a family.
You were his sister and will always be.

He Brought Healing

Loria, what you fight,
God is fighting it for you tonight.
You can rest in him,
the comforter, he'll send to you again.

He'll take care of you;
He sent Angels too.
Jarvis is there, and he said to tell you
he's free, and he comes to see you.

He will always be
in the spirit. He can come anytime and see.
He can travel anytime he wants to.
That is what Angels do.

He came to visit you,
and he brought healing too.
He brought it just for you,
Laura, now you're healed too.

— *Jarvis*

Mamma I'm Coming to See You

I just got my new wings.
I'm learning to fly,
and I'll be coming by
as soon as I

get used to my wings,
these two feathered,
beautiful things.

Now I can come
see you,
and mamma, that
is what I am going to do.

I saw you with a heavy heart,
Mom, you did more than your part.
With you I'll always be.
I am more than a memory.

I'll be your heart.
You'll carry me,
because, I am a part of you
that longed to be free.

And now I am.
I can come visit

anytime I want to.
Now I have my wings,
I will come, and see you.

Healing in my wings,
that's what I bring,
and why I came.

– Jon

You Get Back

Praying the Holy Ghost
all over you.
I hope you
can feel it too.

Evil as can be,
you're not fooling anyone,
and you're not fooling me.

God saw what you did.
Lied and called me a friend.
What I'm telling you is that
I was always a friend and true.

A friend you will never be.
That is what God showed me.

So, I let it go.
He picked it up,
and now I know
a whole lot of stuff.

Wrath comes from God,
and vengeance is his.
He said, "You get back
what you give."

Hey There, Tracey

Hey there, Tracey, it's your mom.
God said to tell you it won't be long.
You're going to get up. Believe me it's true,
and I'll be right beside you.

While you sleep in a hospital bed,
I will have my hand on top of your head.
No, it *is* me; it's just Mom.
Close your eyes, it won't be long.

You will get up and be on your way.
Guess who is there to stay?
Yes, that's right. I'll always be with you
until this trial you get through.

Hold your head high. Mom said so.
Her name is Betty Jean, and she had to go.
However, she will always be with you
You carry her in your heart, and
our memories are how we will never part.

She will never leave you;
she's deep inside your heart.
She'll always be right there,
and she is saving you a spot.

She is alive and well, you see. It's true.
She is waiting in Heaven for you,
a spirit now, and she is by your side,
a Heavenly being, she will never die.

Tracey Durham This Blessing is Just for You

Two percent of your blood is getting to your brain.
In the year 2000, my mom's was just the same.
100 on one side 98 on the other.
He said, "Girls, you had better pray for your mother."

Tracey Durham, he said 99 and 99.
Funny how Mom's turned out just fine.
18 years is what it's been.
I hope Mom never has to go through that again.

Sitting up talking, now that is how God is,
and that is what he will do, because we ask him to.
Most of all, because he loves you,
and this is just the beginning of what he's going to do.

Hold on . . . A blessing is coming, it's true.
You will know, because it's just for you.
It's something only God can do,
and Tracey Durham, this blessing's just for you.

To My Special Family

Nothing can change the way you loved me.
I was special to you, and you are special too.
Mom, I sure love you.

You were my family, and I was so loved,
you *must* have come from the Father above.
I was good-looking. The girls would stare,
and you had my pictures everywhere.

Mom, even though you can't see me around,
deep in your heart, I can always be found.
The fish that is mounted up on the wall
Reminds you how I loved fishing Y'all.

The boat in the backyard—another memory of me.
Thanks for doing that, it's special, and see,

Mom, I know you fought for me for years.
Thank you, Mom, please don't shed any more tears.
Dearest Dad, I love you too. Without you
and Emily, my life would have sure been blue.

You all made me happy, Dad. It wasn't your fault.
Thanks for loving me, and for all that I was taught.

Jessi loved me, and I loved her,
but that wasn't a secret; everyone had heard.
She was my girl, and I'll always be around.
Jessi look, I'm an angel now!

I want to thank you for all that you have done.
You were my family, and I was your son.
I'm here in Heaven looking down on you, see.
I'm saving you all a spot right beside of me.

The Lord, he came and got me. I didn't even know,
but when Jesus took me by the hand, it was my time to go.
Goodbye for now, Emily, Mom, and Dad.
I am waiting here in Heaven, and I am so glad.

Deep within your hearts, and deep within your souls,
know that I am with you wherever you should go.
My memories will never die. My spirit is alive!

The King

Satan offered Jesus everything:
a smorgasbord was laid before our king.
Temptation Satan tried to bring.
Jesus said, "I love God more than anything."

Jesus knew exactly whom he served.
He knew Satan would get what he deserved.
A king and a kingdom, see?
God prepared a place for us to be.

I know you've been hearing that for years.
Well, friends, it's true.
He told me, and he'll tell you too.

Turn away from sin.
God will soon be back again.
Repent!
And don't turn back to sin.

If you do,
You'll be sorry in the end.

I'm Up Here in Heaven

I'm up here in Heaven.
Everything is okay.
The wind is blowing.
The temperature's always the same.

He is the light, and it is always day.
I just wanted to say,
I missed you today.
I saw you writing letters from Heaven—
from me.

Terri, that is what sets you free,
writing it down and letting it out,
venting with sometimes a shout.
I know that you're okay, and
I'll see you again on another day.

I will be coming your way.
It might just be today.
You never know
which way my wings the wind will blow.

Right now, I have to go.
I have many other people to see, you know?
I mean the rest of my family,
but I'll be back, you watch and see.

I Left on the Wings of an Angel

I left on the wings of an angel today.
Nothing could have been stranger, no way.
She came to me,
Took me by the hand and said, "Come and see."

So I took that Angel's hand,
and she had a great plan.
She swooped down picked me up
to take me home, and I was not alone.

I want you all to know that I am okay.
I didn't know I was leaving today,
but I will always be with you
in your hearts and memories too.

I was more than a memory,
and God,
took me home to be
with the King of Kings.
I have need of nothing.

I miss you lots, but it is okay.
I'll be sitting there with you and May.
You see, what has happened to me
is just Gods Glory.

Don't cry tears for me.
This is where I longed to be.
If you wait and see,
I'll be in the spirit and we

can spend time together now.
I'm now a spirit, and I'll come down,
flying high, flying low,
you never know which way I'll go.

Just know that I still love you,
and all you have to do is close your eyes,
and I'll always be with you.

Always in your heart,
I will be, and no one can ever take that from you or me.
I'll be with you wherever you go;
Look deep in your heart, and you will know

— *Dena*

To My Sweetest Girl

Hey Donna, it's me.
And I will never leave.
I'll be in your heart, and memories,
and I'll live forever, you see.

To my sweetest girl:
Honey, you are my world.
I wanted you to have everything.
Blessings I will bring.

I will never leave.
I will never go.
This old world is hard,
and *that* I surely know.

I will be with you.
I am a spirit now.
When the wind blows,
I'll swoop down.

Now I have wings,
and Donna, I can fly!
Don't you worry,
I'll be coming by.

I have two white, feathered,
beautiful wings.
They will be covering you,
and I'll be here too.

All you have to do
is close your eyes,
and I will be with you.
I have wings; I can fly.

You Worshipped Me

Hey there, Tracey.
It's a very special thing
when confirmation
God does bring.

He said he is going to heal you, hon.
That is just the beginning.
It will not be long, and it will be done.

He has his hand on you,
and when it's all done,
the Devil will be through.
Victory will be won.

It's for me, not for you,
and because of your faith,
you *will* pull through.

I am right here.
Moreover, I am the King.
The sickness on you,
glory it will bring.

Everyone will know
when it is over, you see,
that through it all,
you worshiped me.

I Did Not Know

I did not know
it was time to go.
I didn't want to leave,
but God came, see?

My pain is over.
My days are now great.
Trust me, God is never late.

Always on time,
He will always be.
He took time
to come, and get me.

He is the keeper of my soul.
I'm with him now, and
I will never let go.

Heaven is where I am.
God had a great plan.
He took me to my mansion far away,
and this is where I long to stay.

So, know that I didn't leave you.
As a spirit I will always be
in your heart, and even your soul.
Hold me there, and never let me go.

I'm home, and I'm free.
The world can't take it from me,
so I want to tell you this:
I'll be back with a hug, and a great big kiss.

— Jarvis

Jessi and Ash

Jessi's test came back today:
normal.
That's God's way.

We prayed, and he came through.
Baby, He'll always watch over Ash and you.

He said, "Ask," and I did
along with many prayer warriors, that is.

One's name is Loria.
She is family,
like Mom, and she's Mom's little girl,
like me, she always will be.

My children have much prayer.
They pray too, and they care.
They're just like me.
They love the Father thankfully.

The Lord He Is My Shepherd

The Lord, he is my shepherd.
He said I shall not want,
and if I ask him to forgive me,
then want I surely don't.

No matter what happens,
I can always count on him.
He sticks closer than a brother,
and he is closer than any friend.

Yes, I sure do love him.
He shed his blood on the cross.
Without that day at Calvary,
our souls would sure be lost.

So, thank you my sweet Jesus
for what you've done for me,
and if we will repent,
then he will set us free.

I Rolled the Stone Away

When they lay me in the tomb,
there I stayed.
Three days later
I rolled the stone away.

That is when I left.
That is when I went away
to my Father's house,
and there I'll always stay.

I will send the comforter
whenever you need me to,
when no longer can you make it,
I will carry you.

In my Father's house are many mansions.
I've told you this before.
I'm waiting for you in Heaven.
I'm knocking at your door.

I see the Crystal River
flowing from the Thone.
The angels came and got me,
and my Father took me home.

— *Jesus*

If But One Friend

Know when times seem awful,
they're really not so bad.
What if you were stuck in bed? Well,
dang, your life would sure be sad.

I know this is true,
because it happened to me.
You really have it good.
I hope this you can see.

When you get up,
and your legs don't work anymore,
this is when life seems awful,
and just to move is a chore.

When you're paralyzed,
and friends just can't be found,
it seems that life is ended,
and the tears come streaming down,

that's when the ones who love you
will come and sit with you,
and if but one friend stops by,
then you know that they loved you.

If you only have one friend come by,
then you know that friendship is true.
I had a friend who loved and visited me,
and his name is Todd P'Pool.

— Jarvis

Wendy

To my dearest Wendy:
I love you, yes, it's true.
I want to thank you
for everything you used to do.

You never told me no;
instead you just said yes.
I want you to know,
Wendy, you are the very best.

You took me everywhere—
never complained at all.
You were so special,
the most special friend of all.

I love you, my dear Wendy.
You were always my kind and special friend.
I will always love you dearly,
you who were there until the end.

I know that when you get here,
God will let you through,
for always helping me,
and just for being you.

Look toward your future.
Forget about the rest.
We had a good time, Wendy.
You can look back on that.

Goodbye for now, sweet Wendy.
I'll watch over you.
I'm an angel now.
May all your dreams come true.

— Jarvis

It's Not About the Clothes I Wear

It's not about the clothes I wear
nor the way I wear my hair.
It isn't about my diamond rings,
my house, my car, or material things.

It's a matter of the heart —
wait a minute, let me start —
Man looks at the outside;
God looks on the in.

And it doesn't matter what you have
if you're not pleasing him.

Material things will fade away,
but matters of the heart? They stay.
Memories fade away.
You remember them on another day.

It's kind of like old friends: you may
forget them when you're old,
but in the end become their friend again.

It all comes down
to living without sin
and where your treasures are.
Mine are up in Heaven
somewhere beyond the stars.

Do you know where yours are?
Your treasures, that is.
Mine are up in Heaven,
And they're sealed by a kiss!

My Lawyer Said

My Lawyer said, "There will be no more
courtroom lies."

God has seen right past their disguise,
and he saw through all their lies.
Never were you fighting *me*. Sorry, guys!
You have to answer to him, for all your lies!

He said "Justice will be served.
They will get what they deserve.
It's something like a boomerang
that comes back to where it started."

God said, "He isn't dumb,"
just didn't know from where we come,
but you sure will by the time
this lawsuit's done.

God controls the wind, and the waves;
He's in control of everything.

You have no one, but yourself to blame,
and reaping what you sow
will always end the same.
The reason why? God will never change!

Why? Because he gave his only son.
He said, "It's finished — done."

Still, a lot of damage has been done,
but it's okay, because he healed me,
and we won anyway!

And now, Pam and I, we are okay.
We'll move on, and live our lives each and every day.

Thank you, Jesus, for your sacrifice,
and most of all for saving my life.

Discrimination is a problem. It surely was for me,
but God said, "No more will it be."
It is for God's glory, a trial that ends in Victory!

The Night Before Last

The night before last
in my sleep something came.
An evil spirit was to blame.

When I wake up, I say Jesus' name.
It has to go, that's what I know.

Can't fool me, because I know you.
God told me what he'll do.

He will destroy you.
Revelation 20. I thought you knew.

Oh, wait! You did.
He threw you out
along with legions.
Makes me shout!

Now this is how
you get to live. You can't go back.
There's no more doubt.

I know what I am talking about.
"Legions," it says.
I don't want to fight them
while I am in my bed.

Soon, that Devil, and his legions,
He will destroy.
He said he's going to crush them.
Oh, what joy!

I'll say my prayers before I go to bed.
That way that Devil can't get in my head.
I have a bullet made of lead.
I wish I could shoot him and kill him dead.

Hey There, Friend

Hey there, friend. I'm talking to you.
That old Devil has got ahold of you too.
Devil, turn loose of my friend in Jesus' name.
Deliverance — that's the thing.

Why? Because I *believe*.
Therefore, you will receive.
Well, do *you* believe?
Can you even conceive

of what I talk about?
My father, God, he gave his only son,
and salvation that day was won.

Life he gave me
when he died to set us free.

Do you want to be first?
Or do you want to be last?
Why keep looking at the past?

Gone, never to return,
I won't soon forget
the lessons I have learned.

I Sit Here

I sit here, and I wonder how you are.
I hope life's lessons have taken you far.
There's nothing left of where we were,
only friends, that's for sure.

I didn't know that I could pray,
or that God could change it on any given day.
Oh, now I know,
so I pray, and let it go.

Life's lessons I've been taught.
Oh, they have cost me lots.
But now I know what I have got.
Thank you Jesus, it means a lot.

Reaping what you sow
Now I know.
I had to go,
but at least I know.

I wish I could change it all,
but my back was against the wall,
so I decided to change it all.
God delivered me two years ago y'all.

Now I'm free to move on,
let it go and carry on.

Oh, one more thing:
It made me strong.
I know now where I belong.

Seems I Spend My Life Waiting

Seems I spend my life waiting
And now I know
I am waiting on God
And I will continue to wait, so

when it's time
Everything will be just fine.
For my Father
I am always on the frontline

He takes care of me
I trust him
He is closer than a brother.
He is my best friend

I will wait on him anyway.
It's okay;
He has me.
No worries, no more fear,

because my Father is always here,
and I have lost all my fear.
When my Father is standing here,
that old Devil can't get near.

So, I want to share this today:
Jesus is the only way.
Listen to what I say,
and you'll be okay.

Judas

There's a Judas in every bunch.
You may have just taken one to lunch.
Friends are a dime a dozen.
Sometimes, that Judas may even be your cousin.

Friends, that's what they're called.
Life has taught me, y'all,
you have but one true friend
when it comes right down to it,
and that's God.

Humans will let you down.
Sinners have not all yet been found.
Then, you have some who hide
their true evil deep inside

A smorgasbord, they will lay before you.
That's what Satan would have them do.
He has a kingdom too;
it's called Hell, and it is waiting for you.

You can change that today —
send old Judas on his way.
Call on the name of God.
He is the only one that can save us, y'all.

That's about all I've got.
I hope you know I love you a lot.
Oh, and God does too.
He gave his only begotten son for you!

You Wash the Outside

You wash the outside,
what about the in?
If it's dirty
it's gonna work its way out, my friend.

You can only hide that filth for so long,
because you are not that strong.
Only with God is there strength,
and you are not half as smart as you think.

He controls everything,
therefore, give it to him.
Let go of the pain,
and let go of the sin.

He is the only one who can heal.
Ask Him; believe Him, and He will.
Let Him cleanse the inside of you.
He'll destroy that Devil, too.

In the beginning, he already knew
that old Satan was after you.
Give it to God, and it will be through.
He will fix everything for you.

God is Bringing it Down

God is bringing it down.
The good news is spreading all over town.
He has had enough.
He's calling the Devil's bluff.

He said it's just as well.
That Devil is going straight to Hell.
I said it was the good Lord's choice,
and now the devil doesn't have a voice,

nor does he have a chance.
He will dance his very last dance.
Here is his circumstance —
the keys of death and hell at a glance —

a bottomless pit awaits him,
which truly makes me grin.
I hate sin, I can't wait until

my Father comes back again for real.
That Devil will only be loosed for a season.
That's even more of a reason

to get your life right,
because God could come back tonight.
If you're ready, you'll be alright.
Let God in to fight your fight.

An Angel

An Angel came down.
As a matter of fact, she's here right now,
and she'll be back.

She came to visit me,
brought healing virtue, and I'm free.

Some folks just won't listen.
You can tell them over and over again.
They won't listen to you,
Just like they would not listen to Him.

They will wish they did in the end.
They might not get a chance again.
Turn your life around while you still can.
Don't wait until it's too late friend!

Angels unaware—
Friends, they are everywhere
fighting against our sins
until our Father comes back again.

Don't hesitate, and please don't wait.
Hurry up, or it might be too late.
Don't let that Devil, seal your fate.
Don't let the world fill you with hate.

God said "Love,"
from heaven above.
He'll cover you like a glove.
He's the white dove.
Friends, it is all out of love.

He Said, "No More Courtroom Lies"

He said, "No more Courtroom lies."
That's funny! I'm here laughing, guys.
Because it was you who told *all* the lies,
and now you cannot hide.

You must answer for your evil deeds.
I can tell you God isn't pleased.
You better get down on your knees,
and ask Father God, "Father God, please . . ."

Ask him what to do.
He will gladly show you.
And I will too,
because, that is what Christians do.

Well, I don't claim any *particular* religion.
To me, they are just manmade prisons.
The Bible never said be Baptist or Pentecostal.
Some of them are even cults, and to me that is awful.

If in the Word you read it, you will know
these manmade religions, well, they have to go.

There is only the Word.
No matter what I have ever heard.
Many will be deceived

because of something they were told,
or something they believed.

Lord, don't ever let me be deceived again.
Thank you, God, for being my best friend,
and I will see you when
you come back again.

Jesus Christ is the Only Cure

God said to tell you it won't be long.
He'll be coming to take us home.
This world is not where we belong.
He said it won't be long.

You know the answer to
what I'm going to tell you,
and, when I'm through,
you'll know what I know too.

We don't fight against flesh and blood.
You must look past that face that you love.
Discernment is what you need,
so you can try the spirits and see,

and you can make the evil ones flee.
Lord Jesus, keep them away from me.

You can only fight them
with scripture, you see.
It is truth they cannot defeat.
Tell Satan, he can't compete.

That honey dripping from their lips —
Be careful! Don't take a sip!
Seducers — that is what they are.
Remember, spirits too can leave a scar.

If you are fighting tonight,
give it to God to get it right.
The Devil is a deceiver, that's for sure.
Jesus Christ is the only cure!

Loop

He said, "I love you more than anything."
I said, "and I feel the same."
He said, "I love you, and my little girl,
Loop, she's my entire world."

I understand, and that is my kind of man.
That is the kind that only God can make.
He is diligent in every way, and
I would not trade him for anything today

Thankful is all I know.
I told them a long time ago, but
They both already know,
and to be a family is our goal.

God gave them to me,
so we will always be happy, and free.
He said peace and joy.
I love him, he's my favorite boy.

Do you know who I am talking about?
God, without a doubt.
He gave Loop and Eric to me,
and from my past, he set me free.

I couldn't ask for any more.
This is more than I could ever dream for.
He gave it to me,
and the best thing is, it was free.

A blessing for us all three.
Thank you, Father. It is simply

One of the best things
you have ever done for me.
Thank you, Father —
Another victory!

My family is almost complete,
But not until Loop's baby, we get to meet.
Then a larger family we will be.
Oh, Father God is able, and He will do it just for me.

Loop, Too

You are my whole world.
You'll always be Daddy's little girl.
Without you, I wouldn't make it through,
I couldn't, not without you.

I love you so, I tell you the truth,
I don't want bad things to happen to you,
so I warn you stern, because
I want you to learn.

Someday when I'm gone,
my warnings will carry on,
then you'll hear a song
and remember I was never wrong.

I already knew,
because, I have been there too.
So, Loop, I want you to know,
you are my heart and soul.

Remember wherever you go,
I will be with you in the spirit, so

when you can't see me anymore,
shut your eyes and you'll see me soar.

Memories will come through,
and you'll remember all the things
Daddy taught you.

– Eric

I Know a Man Named Freddy

I know a man named Freddy.
Boy, he is ready.
Blades coming out of his fingers.
Mess with him, and it spells danger.

He comes in your dreams.
It is the scariest thing, if you know what I mean.
Real is what it seems,
but wake up, and it was just a dream.

He will cut you with those blades,
those things are sharply made.
A couple of friends he's already slain.
Their lives ended in terrible ways.

A psychopath is what he was,
and it was fake, just a movie y'all.
And when it comes down to it all,
we fight spirits just like him, because

the good Lord said we should do so.
I know it's true, and I know what to do
when they come knocking.
Get gone Devil, or you'll be through.

In the movie you just have to wake up,
but in real life you have to fight that stuff.
It has already been enough,
Freddy, I woke up.

He Said

He said, "I love you."
Well, I loved him too.
Why did he make me wait?
Seems, in the end, he waited too late!

I thought you were great.
I Wish you hadn't made me wait,
and then spirits came, and
some remained.

They wouldn't go,
so now I know how to pray,
and they can't stay.
They have to stay away.

At one time, I didn't know
how to pray,
but now I've learned
how to keep those spirits away.

I wish things could have been different,
but they were not,
so I moved on,
but I loved you a lot.

If you had known the truth,
we could have been free together,
but instead, you wanted to blame me,
so now together we can't be.

I wish you the best.
I hope you have found
what you couldn't find in me.
Someday you'll know the truth,
and will be able to see

that I loved you,
and wanted you forever,
but in the end, that wasn't God's plan, however.

I picked you and didn't wait on God —
a stepping stone to get us to where we are!

She Asked

She asked me if I saw you.
I said, "Who? Do I even know you?"
She said, "Why, yes. You do."
I said, "I don't remember."

She said, "You used to come by all the time."
I said, "I don't remember."
She said, "Remember? You came over
from December 'til December."

I said, "You must be thinking of someone else.
I try to live a quite peaceful life
and stay to myself."

She was someone that I used to know,
but she died, about a year ago.

God said, "No more will they treat you bad."
I said, "Thank you, Jesus, I sure am glad."
Still, it makes me feel a little sad,
but I do not remember you.

Is that bad?
I don't think so, because God said,
"Forget those things which are behind,
Look ahead!"

Oh, Those Spirits!

Oh, those spirits come around.
God is going to knock them down.
I don't know why they don't go on.
They know my Father is on the Throne.

I guess they like to play.
Well I don't play that-a-way.
But I love to see God destroy
all those evil spirits. Oh, what joy!

I know the truth.
It's out the roof,
and I have the proof
that the Devil is a goof.

I'm ready every day
to fight whichever ones come my way,
but I will be glad when its all done.
Thank you God, for sending your son.

This old world sure gets old.
It is a vapor, so I'm told.
It won't last much longer,
since each day I get stronger

Daughter of dust, it won't be long.
I'll be back, to take you home.
Until then, hold onto me.
In the end we'll see victory!

Hello, Son

This is your dad.
I just wanted to say hello,
and I'll always be with you,
wherever you may go.

Hold onto your dreams.
Let go of your fears,
and God will wipe away
all of your precious tears.

Heaven is so wonderful,
not like down here.
I'll be waiting for you,
so son, just don't despair.

Hold on to what I've taught you.
Keep it in your heart
no matter how far away I seem.
I'll be in your heart, and we will never part.

I Fly High

I saw you
when I flew by.
I am an angel now,
and I can fly high.

Oh, and I can fly low.
Depends on
which way the wind blows.

I'm like a butterfly
in the air
up in the sky.
I'll be in the by and by.

Whenever you whisper my name,
shut your eyes and just claim
that I'm still alive, because
your memories are how I survive.

And he's coming back,
in the twinkling of an eye.

Hello, Mom

Hello Mom, it's me.
I was passing by
I looked at you,
and you had tears in your eyes.

Mom it's me.
I came to visit you
even though you can't see me,
this I often do.

I love you so much;
you're so special to me.
I'm sorry I left so soon,
but God came and got me.

I didn't want to leave you,
but God's offer was so great,
I had to go right then.
I couldn't wait.

Mom, I love you dearly
I couldn't have picked a better one, you see,
but I didn't pick you —
God gave you to me.

If I had my pick,
I would still have picked you,
for being a wonderful mom
and just for being you.

– *Jarvis*

Jarvis, Then I Knew

I looked in the mirror and saw you standing there.
I knew it was you, then I saw the glare.
I turned around, but no one was there,
then I saw the outline of your hair in the light.

Jarvis, then I knew you were standing there,
right up by my side.
I knew from that minute on that
you'd be my angel, my own special guide.

I hold onto that outline I saw
in the light. You were standing very tall.
That's when I was sure it was you, Jarvis.
No matter what comes, you'll see me through.

I know that you are with me.
I know it now for sure,
for the reflection in the mirror
showed us hand-in-hand together. Now I know.

Our Riches

Our riches are in Heaven, not down here upon the earth.
If we love the Lord, we'll always put him first;
If we put meat in his storehouse, the riches will come down;
If we know the Lord, then riches we've already found.

Hold onto the Lord with everything you have,
and when all's been said and done, I know that you'll be glad.
He said resist the devil, and he'll have to flee.
Ask the Lord to move that Devil and you can't help but see.

Hold onto the Lord with all your might,
and he will help you fight the good fight
If good seeds we plant, then good fruit we'll bear.
You won't see that Devil around, no, not anywhere.

Call on the name of the Lord, and he will set you free.
If you don't believe it, just take a look at me.
I was a sinner lost, and now at last I'm found.
I gave my life unto the Lord, who turned my life around.

He'll do the same for you that he has done for me.
That's why he gave his only son to die at Cavalry.
I'll say again what I've said before,
Father God is knocking, asking your heart's admittance once more.

I've Missed You So Much

I've missed you so much;
I know you miss me too.
I'm sorry I left;
there was nothing I could do.

You are special to me;
the very most special one,
but it was time for me to go.
My job on earth was done.

I will always love you,
deep down in my soul.
I will be forever with you
wherever you may go.

I'll send you a sign;
you'll know is from me.
I'll visit you often,
though you won't be able to see.

Goodbye for now,
and I love you a lot.
I'm in heaven now,
and I've saved you a spot.

— *Jarvis*

From Heaven, I'm Waiting for You

I am watching over you from Heaven—
me and the angels too.
Don't cry or be sad
there was nothing you could do.

I watched the doctors work on me
They did all they could too.
Please don't be sad because
God has brought me through.

For when you least expect it,
He'll be coming after you.
Until that day comes,
I'll wait right here for you.

Please hold onto the Lord,
and he will see you through.
Then one day you will get here.
Your trials will all be done.

Never again will we part.
This someday when it comes, you'll see.
Open up your heart unto the Lord,
and soon you'll be with me

Hold on to your dreams, but
go on and forget the past.
When we are together,
We'll be together forever at last.

To Mom and Dad

Mom and dad, I love you,
and I'm sorry that I'm gone.
Even though you miss me,
you must carry on.

Thank you for the life
that you have given me,
but I'm not the only one;
you have the other three.

Your grandchildren all need you,
and your great-grandson will to.
When you're feeling down,
I'm still around, watching over you.

You both were always there for me.
You gave up everything.
I had a wonderful life growing up,
and I hope you both had the same.

You were both so special,
and both of you still are.
The things that you have taught me
always took me far.

You're both so special to me,
the best parents, a boy could have.
Every time I thought of you,
it always made me glad.

I will always miss you.
I prayed for you both every day.
Know I always loved you,
but here I want to stay

until the day comes
when I see you both again.

You are my wonderful special parents.
I love you and I'll miss you
until I see you again.

— *Jarvis*

To Tressa

You are the most wonderful sister;
this I hope you know.
I'll be with you wherever you may go.

There is a special place for a sister like you
up in the heavens above the sky so blue.

I love you my dear sister,
and I'll always be here to defend you,
because that's what sisters
are supposed to do, just because I love you.

You're such a special sister,
this I have to say,
you are special in every single way.

Know that you're as good as anyone.
You're the very best.
I love you more than anyone, any of the rest.

Know I'll always defend you
until the very end.
I love you my dear sister,
My dear, dear friend.

I would not trade you for another.
Oh, no, I really would not.
Always know within my heart
you hold a special spot.

No one better ever hurt you.
No, they better not.
I'll be watching over you,
just because I care.

There's one more thing I have to say:
if I leave before you do, you'll make it too someday.

Know I love you, and I thank you
for all you always do.

I Can't Believe You Left Us

I think of you dear brother,
morning, noon, and night.
I can't believe you left us,
and you're now nowhere in sight.

I've looked for you most everywhere.
You were my dearest friend.
I love you my dear brother, and
I wish you'd come back home again.

You were such a wonderful person;
always loved our mom and dad.
When you went and left us,
all of us were sad.

I know it's just so selfish,
but I want you here with me.
I thought you'd always be here
and never have to leave.

Now I realize in my heart
that you are really gone,
but in my mind I can't believe
you're never coming home.

I hold onto the memories every single day,
and now you've gone to heaven,
so everything's okay.

We Went to Mom's Today

We went to Mom's today.
Me and Tress were on our way.
Little Bitty, took us there
(I love that little car),
but why do people stare?
They do it everywhere.
Because my sister is so beautiful.
Now, that right there
could be why, they all stop and stare.
Her beauty, well, none can really compare.
Like Mom, it's in her genes.

Mom was a looker too,
and she loved her diamond rings.
Thing is God gave that all to her,
and this is how I know
Jewelry is not that bad
long as you don't put it before the Lord.
He'll make a way for you to have it.
Mom's, an example to me.
She's lived it every day, and
taught me, don't you see?
What is right and what is wrong.
And because she is my mom,
when God comes back,
I'll get to go back home.

That Body You Live In

That body that you live in
is beautiful to me,
but please be careful not to become vain.

That body that you live in
is nothing but a shell
you'll shed one day.
When? None can ever tell.

If you are beautiful in the flesh,
don't let it run your life.
True beauty is on the inside, and it
can't survive in a body full of sin.

If you are ugly on the inside
It won't look pretty on the outside.
All over you will become ugly,
and that is just the truth.

We all must age. We're supposed
to grow old with grace that will
show up on our faces. Wrinkles
earned, and each one is a lesson.

Grow old and be thankful.
Be who you really are.

Those looks, in the end,
Won't get you very far.

No matter who you are, God
created you, and to him,
you are a shining star. Did
that message get through?

If you are vain then this is for you,
and I hope you can see it too.

If you are vain, remember: God's
the potter, and you are the clay.
If you don't do right early in your
life, he can take your beauty away.

I Only Want To

I only want to marry you
if you truly love me — for me.
There can't be any other reason;
that's the only way it can be.

God gave me to you
and you to me.
You are my heart's desire,
and you make me smile.

You are all I could ever want
and nothing more, so don't
you ever think it wasn't
God who put that love right there.

It is true and unconditional. Do you see
what you mean to me? One day
you'll know me all the way
to the depths of my very soul.

So, here we go with God beside us,
as our faithful guide. Our life together
will always be exciting
as a homerun slide.

He and I, we know why.
We'll take a lifelong joy ride
with you right by my side,
always sure about who
poured this love into our hearts.

And because it's founded on bedrock,
the blessings will keep on coming,
and they will never stop!

Oh, Look—What a Mess!

Oh, look—what mess!
Things sometimes happen like this.
Now it's sealed with a kiss,
and they'll no longer treat us like this.

You and your husband
are simply hypocrites.
God said I should to tell you
He doesn't like this.

He said when his wrath
comes down upon you,
Oh, the damage he will do!

Reaping what you sow,
His vengeance is coming for you,
and for your husband too.

He messed up a long time ago,
but he and I both already know,
and I have let it go. But look out!
A boomerang comes back to land its blow.

I'm praying mercy for the both of you.
I think you're going to need it.

I told God, and he said, "Terri I know.
I picked it up a long, long time ago.
Now it's up to me, so
like you said, just let it go."

I said, "Okay God,"
and I prayed for both of y'all.
In the end, he said, "Pray no more.
It's over. I'll settle the score."

A Snake in the Grass

The thing is,
God is much stronger than Satan.
If you're waiting on Satan,
you'll keep on waiting.

He is the father of lies,
the author of confusion.
Let him in, and
it won't be an illusion;
it will be the conclusion.

He may be the prince of the powers of the air,
the ruler of the world,
but he does not scare
this little girl.

I live in my Father's world,
and I'll always be His little girl.
He takes care of me, and
all I have to do is rebuke Satan
to make him flee.

A snake in the grass—
be careful as he goes past.
He'll never be first,
but with him, you are always last.

Put it behind you
and just repent.
You'll be glad
it was an angel, God sent.

I Never Have to Worry

If you live to eat
you're going to die.
If you eat to live,
then you'll survive.

That's why I'm alive.
I read the Bible,
and get full inside,
then I testify.

It is food for your soul.
It'll help you
wherever you go.

How do I know?
Because
God lives in my soul.

My soul, it is well,
no matter how my flesh appears.
Father God
is standing right here.

He takes care of me.
I never have to worry.
He's the keeper of my soul.
It's him, not me, wherever I go.

He Passes You By

I love the good,
and I had the wrong
that kind of sounds like a song.

God's not deaf.
He can hear you when you call.
The thing is, your sins can cut you off.

He turns his face from you;
that is what sin causes God to do.

Evil, is why you may not find
God's blessings upon you,
so let that be a lesson.

You roar like hungry bears.
Murder is everywhere.
You moan with mournful cries,
but God simply passes you by.

Cut off from God you'll certainly be.
That's what God said, see?
Better change today;
He'll soon be on his way.

We Are Like Taxicabs

We are like taxicabs.
They transfer from one to the other,
and that's bad.

We carry them here and there,
and they jump on and off.
They don't care.

Spirits, evil ones, that is.
Let God handle it,
because that's his biz.

I give it all to him.
I am at his feet,
and that's why
my life is now complete.

Peace and Joy — I have both now.
God is my best pal.
He said I'm his gal.
I'm going home
but I get to stay here for now.

He fights the evil spirits for me
when they come.
He fights them and I stay free.

That's how it will always be.
God takes care of me.

We Are Right

He sent us to fight this fight.
They are wrong,
and we are right.

Pam, he said to tell you,
we win, and they are through.

June, is what he said.
Wow! I thought
when the email I read

said June 21st.
That devil,
he cannot curse
me or you,
because he sure has tried to.

God is fighting our fight.
It's a simple case of
black and white.

He fights our fights for us,
takes care of all the evil stuff,
and turns it around.
Glory to God! Justice is found.

I See It

I see it everywhere I turn,
only God can make me strong.
When I am weak in the flesh,
well, I don't have to worry about that.

He takes care of it, see? He takes care of me.
That is why I am free. He paid the price,
so we *all* could be

free to choose which road we'll take.
I'll pass on the world, its simply fake.
Come on, give me a break,
I know you not, and I can't relate.

Fake, I want no part,
and the world is full of it, y'all.
I'll enjoy a quiet, peaceful life
beside my family, to be precise.

That will be really nice.
God has already shown me twice.
I claimed it with Theresa that day,
and it'll be our house by August, I'd say.

I claimed it as I drove away.
I've believed it ever since that day.

I won't forget what all she said.
I pray for her before I go to bed.

What I saw that morning was joy;
it was overflowing, unspeakable,
and full of Glory.

She shared it with me —
God's going to give us that house for free,
Because I claimed it to be
ours, he will do it for me.

Simply because I believe, and
He said "ask and you'll receive,"
that is what I did, so
in that house we'll get to live.

My Pearls

I gave away some of my pearls today.
Every day that's my way,
so this I will say:
thank you, Jesus, for making me this way.

Thank you, for letting us share
what we know.
We share it along the way
dropping seeds wherever we go.

Share the good news friends:
Jesus Christ is coming back again.

My friend and I, we prayed,
then, she was on her way.
She couldn't stay,
But God healed her anyway.

Oh, and her boyfriend too—
deliverance for both of you.
The Holy Ghost will come through
Robin, and do what we have asked him to.

— *Terri*

Robin

You are as beautiful
as can be.
It's on the inside
and outside you see.

Don't let anyone tell you anything else.
God made you all by himself.

He said, you are his,
and, what you do, and where you go
is his biz,
simply because you are his.

Real beauty comes from within.
Just let me begin:
a loving heart full of faith
God said none can erase.

The gifts and beauty he's given you,
it's for his glory,
and that is the truth.

His light shines right through,
and Robin, it is shining on you.
He will get you through
just because he loves you.

She Will Always Be

She will always be evil;
she is of the world.
She is nothing more
than a home-wrecking old girl.

But God said, "No more,"
and right now, he is settling the score.

He's heaping hot coals, upon her head;
if she isn't careful, she'll end up dead.

That is the price for sin.
And what she said?
I lose no sleep over it
when I lay down my head.

She'll reap the harvest
she has sown,
face the lessons, she never learned.

Her husband will someday be gone,
and she'll be left all alone
as a dog, to its vomit, it returns,
in a world where you'd think she'd learn.

No one to come, no one to care,
they'll all say leave that old girl there.

But I will still pray
that she changes anyway.
God help her if there's any hope.
That is all I have to say

It will be Gods way.
I gave it to him, and
I'm free of it today.
There was no other way.
Remember, my Father does not play.

Don't Let Those Evil Men

Don't let those evil men
trample on me.
Don't let their wicked hands
Push me around.

Look! They have fallen,
they have fallen now.
God threw them down.
They will not get back up again.

They are haters,
filled with greed and sin.
They will be destroyed in the end.
I tell you now

He said He'll pay you back.
The cup you met me with
is coming back.

You'll now be trampled
as you trampled me.
God said be still,
and he will let me see.

That gives me no pleasure—
none at all—

but it's your own fault,
you shouldn't sin and fall

short of the glory
that could be upon you,
but instead, greed
has taken you over, too.

In the end, you will leave
the same way as me,
and you can't take your money with you.
Naked you will be.

When you leave,
you'll turn back to dust like me.
Back to dust, where you came from, see?

In August

In August, you can move in with me.
I'll buy the house,
and you get to live there for free.
The best part is that you get to be with Loopy and me.

Donnie, he can too.
Donnie Parrent, that basement
is open always to you.

I'll take care of everyone.
We will all have unlimited fun,
and, when it is done,
a nice, quiet, peaceful life, we will have won.

The keys to the kingdom, you see,
Eric, He gave them to you and to me.
We can live there,
and we will do so until eternity.

Me, you, and Hunter too.
That is exactly what we're going to do.
Donnie, that invitation is always open to you.
We are just waiting on you.

You also have an acre or two
for whatever you want to do.
It is up to you!

Daddy, I Need You

Daddy, I need you in this world.
I have needed you since I was a little girl.

My world would not be the same.
I cannot, even contain

a thought of you being gone.
Mom, would be alone,

so, I asked God, to heal you.
He said he was thinking of that too.

He controls everything, and because I have asked,
That is what he's going to do,
Daddy, he is going to heal you,

So, Daddy, Happy Father's Day to you
from me and Tressa too.
Daddy, we love you.
Oh, and Momma does too.

None of us
can make it without you,
so I told God,
and, he's going to see you through.

I Know a Place

I know a place
where I can go
when I'm feeling sad or low.

It is magical and beautiful to me.
It's my imagination.
It creates a vision for me to see.

Anything goes where I am at.
It is all about my Father.
Don't worry about that.

He comes to me in one second flat.
I worry about nothing,
because God knows right where I am at.

He goes before you and me,
because I ask him to, you see.
When I arrive, peace is already there.
My Father, he sends it where

I am headed.
God bless me,
and God bless you.

He Left for Heaven Recently

He left for Heaven recently.
I thought he'd be healed, but
well, he is, you see.
Now he's with our little baby.

I bet our baby boy met him at the gate.
You know our baby wasn't one second late.
And remember, Jesus met him too,
and said, "Hey, your baby boy
has been waiting on you."

Now you are healed, and that cancer is gone.
When you left, God took you home.
There is no cancer where he's at;
he has already forgotten about all of that.

We'll have no memory in Heaven.
Former things will pass away.
When he left for Heaven,
God healed him that very day.

He was completely healed.
That is simply God's will,
so all the prayers I prayed
must have helped in some kind of way.

I thought you'd be healed today,
but God healed you a different way.
He came and got you and took you with him.
There'll be no more pain or chemo ever again.

I'm okay. I'm right here,
your angel, always near.

Never again will you be afraid.
God came, and now you have it made.
That was my main prayer,
that no matter what happened here,
you would make it there.

We were always good friends.
We didn't make it, but that isn't a sin.
We'll talk about it all when I get there, old friend.

He Was My Uncle Buddy Y'all

He was my Uncle Buddy y'all.
We'd go to Cincinnati to see him,
and we always had a ball.

A convention is what it was called.
They cooked all kinds of food.
Buddy, anyone could call,
and the Holy Ghost soon would fall.

The Holy Ghost would fall,
and those women would run.
I have never had so much fun.

He clothed the needy,
and fed the poor.
No one could ask for anything more.

The best preacher I ever knew,
Uncle Buddy,
that was you.

I miss you so much,
and I can't wait to see you again—
a great preacher and a great friend.

Mom came down from upstairs.
She said, "There are angels everywhere—
to the rafters of that Church."
Buddy, always put God first.
He loved God the most.

Ask me how I know,
because I know what I saw.
My Uncle Buddy
was full of the Holy Ghost y'all.

If you didn't know him here,
you'll get to know him there,
because my Uncle Buddy,
he spread the word and didn't care.

As long as he was working for his King,
he knew God would take care of everything.

Death Came Because of Adam and Eve

Death came because of Adam and Eve.
They ate that apple; Satan deceived.
God said, "You'll work for your food,
and she'll have babies. Suffering you will do."

Punishment for their sins,
and we're still paying for it,
and will until God comes back again.

God cursed the ground,
so they would work hard,
or else no food would be found.

Satan came in the form of a snake.
He's so fake, make no mistake.
He still comes that way today
in many forms and many ways.

So, try the spirits and see
if they are like Adam and Eve.
If they are, go on ahead and pray.
God will create a way to escape.

Perfect Love Cast Out Fear

Perfect love can cast out fear.
Don't you know
there isn't any here?

I know who *I* fear,
and God always cares.
He always knows,
because before me he always goes.

He is the beginning and the end.
I have told you this before, dear friend.
Don't wait until it's too late,
or Hell will be your fate.

So hurry up and call
on the Master, all.
He will come to you
as soon as you ask him to.

Ask, and if you can believe,
then your miracle
you will receive.

I already know.
He gave us Marlei, so
no one can tell me God doesn't heal.
She's our miracle, if you will.

She was so early,
but God showed me
if we would pray,
we would see a miracle that day.

That is exactly what we saw.
Our Marlei, is a miracle you'll.

The Devil Has to Quit

You will bow before him.
We all will be your friends,
and, in the end,
Glory will begin.

I can't wait for the eastern sky
to split wide open
before my eyes.

Then that trumpet will sound.
I hope salvation you have found.
It will be over in the twinkling of an eye.
Don't make God pass you by.

He will come, and He will go.
It'll be quick; He said so.
You better know right now,
God is bringing sin down.

Multibillion Dollar Corporations will fall,
I know! Because He said so y'all.
Oh, that is not it.
When we get to Heaven,
that Devil has to quit.

That House is Pending

That house is pending for the second time.
I certainly believe that house is mine.

I was driving along,
and I got lost.
I started praying, and when I looked up—

I had said Lord, take me home—
I felt scared, and all alone.

I was so glad he heard my prayer.
I looked up, and that house was right there.

I drove right up to the garage.
I couldn't believe it; there it was.

The next thing I know,
Theresa said, "God has a miracle for you,

it is coming down the road."
"That is the truth," I said, "I know."

She said, "Claim it." I said, "I already did."
And in that house, my family is going to live.

I saw it twice, I'll see it again,
and, that will be the 3rd time, friend.

I said, "I'll see you at the bank,"
and she said, "that is right."

We claimed it as I drove away.
I believe it is already mine anyway.

I asked God, so I believe it will be mine.
My future and my family are going to be fine.

Those Tumors Dissolved

God said, "Did you ask me
to heal your little girl?"

"Yes, Father I did."
He said, "The good news is
Hunter is going to live."

He said, "Didn't I show you?
Those tumors dissolved."
I said, "Yes, you did, Father God."

He said, "I cannot lie.
I am God, and that is why

"I chose Hunter to be a vessel for me,
because I know that she
loves me, and that is how it will always be.

"She is my girl, don't you know?
I'm the one who made her,
and I'll decide when its time for her to go."

"But for now,
I'm leaving her there on Earth with you,
and her Daddy too,
because you believed me when you ask me to.

"You asked me over and over again to heal your little girl,
and because of that,
she won't be needing healing anymore!

"Why? Because, I am the King,
and I decide everything!

"So I will let her stay, and she will be okay.
It will be my way. Pray without ceasing every day."

"Thank you, Father, that is what we will do.
We will pray without ceasing, and give it to You."

— Jesus & Terri

One Soul

Our souls can intertwine,
and then we can unwind.
Then we can intertwine our souls again.
I love you, and you are my best friend.

One day I'll marry you.
Intertwine our souls is what we'll do.
There is no one I'd rather intertwine souls with than you.
You will always be my dream come true.

Oh, and I love you, and my love is true.
It is only for you, and our little Hunter too.
Do you want to intertwine souls with me?
Okay, then, that is how it will be
You will be one soul with me!

– Terri

Let Me Attack Carolyn

Satan arrived with the Angels.
God said, "Why are you here?"
He said, "I have been watching everything
from down there.

"Let me attack Carolyn
and take away her health,
and I want to steal
all of her Daddy's wealth."

So God said,
"Satan, you go right ahead
Carolyn will hold onto me,
and that is written in letters of red."

So that devil went,
and all manner of sickness and disease
Satan sent.

They said Mom wouldn't live about 20 times,
but guess what? Because of God, Mom is going to be fine.

I asked God to heal my Mom and Dad.
He said, "It is time," and He'd be glad

to do that for me,
because I asked, and I believed.

God said, "It is almost time.
Carolyn, she is mine.

"I'll heal her in my time.
Like Job, Carolyn will be fine."

My Master

He's my master;
I am his slave.
He blesses me every day.

He came to serve,
and that is what we are supposed to do:
serve Him, and He'll bless you,

put you first every day,
and lead you along your way.
A path of light,
no darkness in sight.

Yes, He is the one.
He and I have so much fun,
and when God is done,
victory will be won.

Come on and join the fun,
because my Father is almost done.
He gave His only Son,
so that war is already won.

The Holy Ghost Stays

I've never loved anyone
like I love you.
What did you do?

Oh! I know, and I can see
exactly what you have given me.

Thank you, Lord, I'm so thankful today
that you sent me his way,
and for all you've done,
especially for giving your only Son.

You have blessed me
in so many ways,
every time You do, I'm still amazed,
so I'll keep on giving You all of the praise.
That way, the Holy Ghost stays.

Just Like Job

My mom is just like Job.
She has suffered so much,
but still holds on.

He said, it won't be long,
so she'll always hold on
to the Master, to the King,
because of that healing He will bring.

See, that's the thing,
it's just like a boomerang
If you sling it,
whatever you send, it brings back.

You better sow good seeds
and do good deeds.
With you, I pled,
don't let Satan deceive.

God Asked Satan

God asked Satan, "What are you doing here?"
He said, "I have been watching
everything going on out there,

"And if you will let me attack
your servant Job, no longer will he serve."
God said, "Satan, what nerve.
Job will always serve.

"Go ahead, Satan, attack.
Job will never turn his back.
Just don't kill him when you attack.

"Do whatever you want,
but don't kill him."

So that Devil attacked Job, and
he lost everything. The Bible says so.

He had sores all over him,
cut them with glass, and wiped ashes on them.
He lost all he had,
but in the end,
God made Satan give it all back—

Way more than he stole.
I know, because the Bible says so,
and because of my mom.
Like Job, no matter what, she holds on.

Now I Understand

Now I understand.
It comes down the vine.
Cut it off
while there is still time.

Can't you see?
Your sins come down the vine to me.
It wants to destroy you all three.

Generation after generation,
it continues down.
Our sins fall upon our children,
Like right now.

You have to pray
for God to cut it off now.
He will break that vine,
and when He does that for you,
Taylor will be free, and Steph will too.

And Joelen, that is what He said, to tell you.
And He is going to break that vine for you.
Pray without ceasing, and He will take care of it.
No longer will Taylor or Steph do those things;
they will simply quit.

Momma, Please Don't Cry

Momma, I have wings,
and I can fly.
I can do anything,
and I live in the sky.

My wings are large
and in charge.
These things are as big as a barge.

I fly high, and I fly low.
You never know which way
these wings will go.

But there is one thing
I know: I love you, Momma,
and I'm sorry I had to go.

It isn't that spider's fault.
I just happened to be lying where it walked.

It was an accident.
When it happened, angels God sent,
and that's when I went.

Momma, I'm waiting on you.
You'll be here one day too.

Know my love was true.
There is not another mom
I'd pick over you.

I am okay. I'll always be around.
Lots of memories and happiness found.
Momma, I'm an Angel now.
I'll come see you; you were my favorite gal.

Momma, please don't cry.
Don't worry I am alive.
I'm home with Jesus, you see,
Him, and the Angels came and got me.

— *Little Ray*

Momma

I went by to see (Brother) today.
I saw him, but his spirit was away.
He was with the Father today,
no matter what they say.

His body is resting.
His spirit is gone.
It'll come back to him,
when his flesh is strong.

He will tell you when he wakes up
what he saw.
It's in the spirit
He told me to tell y'all.

— Little Ray

Momma, Too

I came by to see you.
You were sleeping,
and I was watching over you,
because that is what the angels do.

My wings cover you with love,
like a feather bed,
white as a dove.

It's love that comes from above.
I brought healing with me
in my wings,
and I am free.

Momma, I saw you cry.
Please, Momma, dry your eyes.
I am free as I can be.
That old devil, had to flee.
Now he can't touch me.

"I'm waiting for you,"
he said, "to tell you
your healing will come,
and when it's over, Victory
you will have won."

— *Little Ray*

Hey There, Wendy

Hey there, Wendy, it's just me.
Me and Little Ray, are hanging out, you see.

We came to see you, but you were sleeping, so sound,
My wings covered you, when I came down.

Every tear that you have cried,
they are bottled up
in a little vile on the other side.

He saves them up 'til you get home.
You won't travel home alone.

He will turn those tears to joy,
and one day before you know it,
you'll be back with your boy.

Until then, I'll be watching out for him.
We play Ted, every now and then.
And Wendy, I can sing now, my friend!
LOL, I wish we could do that again.

We had lots of fun.
We would ride, and
I would sing.
You may have cried!

Up here in Heaven, me and Little Ray
play air guitar, and the angels sing
"Amazing Grace."

Wendy, it's just me, Jarvis.
Me and Little Ray dropped by to see
how you are, and how you've been. Dear friend,
I love you, and I'll take good care of him.

— Jarvis

Back in Grade School

Back in grade school,
in second grade, I met my best friend.
One day, she came to the whirler
with an ice cream in her hand.

I said, "Where did you get that,
Loria Ann?"
She said, "I stole it."
I said, "You can't!

"You can't steal.
You'll go to Hell!
Take it back right now!"

So, off we went.
Miss Polley was Heaven-sent.

We took it back and gave it to her,
and back to the whirler we did go.
It wasn't long before mom was missing quarters.
I said, "It was not me, Momma."

Then finally, I told the truth.
Mom, she cut loose, that was it.
This little hypocrite, she quit.
And that was it.

I didn't know I was a hypocrite,
but that day I learned it.
Let that be a lesson to you in life:
Hypocrites come in all kinds of sizes.

Hey, Lennie

Tony, would bring a little brown bag of candy
and all the girls would drool, you see.
One of those girls
just happened to be me.

We all wanted to be his girl for the day.
He'd share his candy that-a-way.
He was a great friend, too.
Back in eighth grade the things we'd do!

Candy was our favorite thing —
all the goodies, Tony, would bring.
It won't be the same —

Oh, wait! A message just came through.
He said he'll be coming by.

He is an Angel now,
and he can fly, and I'll tell you how.
Well, Lennie, Tony, has wings.
They are huge, white, fabulous things,

like a great big feather bed,
dove white, fell on his head.
The feathers ran down, and he now has wings —
two big, white, beautiful things.

They glitter and sparkle
and can light up your way.
Tony said to tell you that he's okay.
He's on his way, and he'll stop by, and say,

"Hey Bro, it's me.
It's your Brother, Tony.
I just came by to watch over you.
I am an Angel now, and
all my dreams have come true.

"Hey, I miss you
and all the things we used to do.
Just remember, I didn't leave you.
I'm an angel now, and I'm as good as new.
It's Tony, tell Pam too, one day I'll see both of you."

Happy Father's Day Daddy

Daddy, Happy Father's Day to you.
I sure do love you too.
A Daddy and a son have a bond, it's true,
and Daddy, no one can ever
break the bond I have with you.

Daddy, Happy Father's Day to you.
No other Daddy would ever do.
I'd trade no other Daddy for you.
Daddy, I'm just glad God picked you.
Remember, you gave me that shotgun and a .22?
Daddy, I'll pass them down to Loopy Loo.
She sure loves you too.
And Daddy, I want to thank you.

Daddy, we used to drink and play cards
down at Gracie's Bar.
Back in the day, to Gracie's we'd go
to drink Cokes and play pool, you know.
I have so many good memories of you.
Daddy, what would I do,
if anything ever happened to you?
So I pray, and God always lets you stay,
and here you are, on another Father's Day.
That is just God's way, since I ask him, every day.

Daddy, all those things were fun we used to do.

I remember you'd come through,

and give us all a five-dollar bill,

and Daddy, you're giving still.

You bailed me out when no one would.

Thank you, Dad; you always understood.

Oh, and thank you Daddy, for that Mercury of sky blue.

I loved that car, and the wooden arm rests too.

Daddy, no one could do what my Daddy could do.

Yes, I am talking about you.

So, Daddy, thank you, and Happy Father's Day.

I hope you'll get to stay here on Earth.

I ask God every day, and He says He hears.

If I keep praying, He'll add plenty of years.

Wendy, Today We Celebrate *Me*

Wendy, today we celebrate *me*.
I love all of my family,
but today's reserved just for me.
God, knew exactly when I would leave.

To the Father, I have cleaved,
and the other day he showed me
Heaven where I'd be.
He said, sweet memories, I am free.

Free to fly, away up high,
and I will never die,
because Jesus gave his life.
My spirit is alive.

And I will always be
alive, eternally.
My spirit, it is free.
So, Wendy, don't cry for me.

A celebration, of my life
this day will be.
Don't be sad and know I'm here.
To you, my spirit will always be near.

Celebrate *me* today.
I'm really not gone away.
I'm in my Father's house to stay,
and my spirit will visit you every day.

I will only be gone a little while.
One day you'll come home too, and then
we both will smile.
A great reunion, it will be.
You'll be home in Heaven with me.

— *Brother*

Wendy

It is a day to celebrate my life.
God came and got me, to be precise.

Today you all celebrate me.
God came and he got me,
and now I'm an angel — Holy — see?

Healed! I am.
Home! In Gloryland.
That is where I now stand.
I cannot wait to see you all again.

I'm up here with Mom and Dad.
Oh, and Little Ray.
We run and play.
We worship the Father all day.

Nothing like down there.
It's like nothing you've ever seen.
Heaven is simply GLORY!

Oh, and Wendy, we are free.
Free as a bird could ever be.
Free just like I longed to be.
Free as the wind, blowing through the trees.

We all three are free.

We're up in Heaven, and we are saving you all a seat.

Nothing on Earth could ever compete.

And when we got to heaven, our healing was complete.

— *Brother*

Hey Wendy, You Know I Like to Fish

Hey Wendy, you know I like to fish
Well, guys, its like this:
He took two fish and fed many, see.
He'll do the same for you or me.

I am now eating at the Master's table.
I ate all my fish, and I saved some for later.

God said, to tell you, He is able,
that there is always plenty of food at *His* table.
He is the head, and He is able,

Wendy, to heal you,
because this angel right here asked Him to.
So, Wendy, your healing will come.
He said, my job on Earth was done.

It is all about God's only begotten Son.
He'll heal your COPD; it will simply go away
with a touch of the Master's hand is what He had to say.

I'll be by to see you, I'm an angel now,
and will always be. That is what God, did for me.
I am free, no more sickness, and all I see is glory.
I am totally healed, and that was my Father's will.

I will be by to see you now and again.

Not only was I your brother; I was your friend.

You know, Wendy, in the end

we will all be together again.

— *Brother*

Hey Wendy, It's Me

Hey, Wendy, it's me. I'm still here.
You cannot see me, but I am near.
The Holy Ghost is also here.
Sweet family, have no fear.

He could not let me stay with you here,
He said, because if He did,
I would be sorry, and so would you all
that God let me live.

Healing, He said, for me,
was Him coming to set me free —
the way it was supposed to be,
and that is what I am. Free.

That's the way I was healed,
and that was my Father's will.
I was loaned to you all for a time,
and now that time is mine.

Up here, I'm having a fresh new life, you see,
Mom, Dad, Little Ray, and me,
and we are as happy as can be.
We have life eternally.

— *Brother*

My Boyfriend and Me

Me and my boyfriend were sitting out back
last night. It must have been around eleven.
It was the craziest thing I have ever seen—
a deer stopped not fifteen feet from him and me.

She stayed there for twenty minutes or more, and
that's when God spoke your brother's name.
And that deer? She remained.

She looked me right in the eyes.
I saw no fear. She was pretty good-sized.
Then God said your brother's name,
and I knew it was your brother's spirit that came.

Wendy, I felt the pure and loving peace
that only comes from God,
who said, "Heaven is where our Brothers are.

"Free and saved from all sin.
Eternity
that will never end.
Until then,
they watch over all of you."

— Terri Johnson

Sparkle, Shine, and Glitter

Wendy, you should see these things!
My great big, white, feathered, beautiful wings.
They are magical, you see, like fairy dust
God poured all over me.

Now I can fly,
and you know why?
Because when God, healed me,
He gave me these beautiful wings.

Now I can fly,
Do you know what that means?
I can come see you, with these
two beautiful things.

Sparkle, shine, and glitter too,
then the light of God shines through.
Wendy, it's even shining on you!
This gorgeous light is going to see you through.

I am not gone. This angel's coming home,
and oh, it won't be long.

I may look like a spirit, see,
but, know that it's just God and me,
and I have come to be with my family.

– *Brother*

Reaping the Seeds You Have Sown

Wendy, you are reaping the seeds that you have sown.
Oh, the lessons you have learned!
All you have done and been through has made you strong.
Wendy, it won't be long.

Joy, and happiness are waiting for you,
and when it's done, you'll know too,
exactly what it all was for, and you got through
because Father God in Heaven carried you.

He said, Wendy, to tell you
as a fine and good servant, you'll surely do.
Wendy, He said He loves you,
and because of all you've done for others,
 He'll do the same for you.

And one day, when you least expect it,
He'll come for you.
He said, "Sweet Wendy, please don't be blue.
I have a treasure chest in Heaven
and it's waiting just for you."

And because of all the good that you have done here,
He wants you to know, He'll always be right there,
and when you need Him, all you have to do is call.
He said He loves you, that you are His little doll.

You are beautiful to Him, and to me.
Both of us love our special Wendy.
Hold your head high, you're a child of the King.
He said, to tell you of the many blessings He'll bring.

He said, you are simply
reaping the seeds that you have sown,
and He has made you strong, Wendy, hold on.
He's coming back, and it won't be long!

Wow, I!

Wow! I walked through those pearly gates.
The angel said to me, "You look great!"
He said, "I had to wait,
but now you're here. God's never late."

In the spirit, I was pain free.
My sufferings were for someone else to see,
for when He came,
no longer did I have any pain.

My body was suffering, but I was not, see?
That part was no longer me!
It was just a shell to wear while I walked on Earth,
but I'm home in Heaven with Jesus now, my friend.

Don't you worry, because, you see,
the angels sing and rejoice over me.
I am now free, my one true love, He came and got me.

Wendy, I'm home, and it is more beautiful than
I could have ever known. I am waiting on
you. Mom, Dad, and Little Ray are too, and
when your job on Earth is through,
Jesus said, He'll come for you.

Sister, hold onto Him;
He will see you through,
and sweet Sister, when you can
no longer make it, He will carry you!

I'm Home Now

I'm home now—no place I'd rather be
than home with Jesus—He came and got me.
The gates are as one giant pearl. I knew that
I was home in one second flat.

Angels sing and rejoice before the King,
God, who can do anything. I sing
before the throne. He came and brought me home.
This is where I belong. It was always my home.

The streets are transparent, pure gold.
The stories are true about Heaven you've been told.
Living waters flow from the King.
No medicine is needed here, since healing, God brings.

I'm home with the morning star,
and I'll be with you wherever you are.
You won't have to look far;
I'll be shining from afar

— *Brother*

Moved On

You've finally moved on,
and so have I.
Sixteen years have passed us by.

I don't know why.
The answers are up in the sky.

One day we'll know exactly why,
and the lessons I have learned
were for you and me alone.

What was this all for?
Stepping stones and nothing more.
Those days are long gone,
but they made us both strong.

I wish you a happy future,
and I'm glad I was once your wife.
I believe you will remarry, this time for life.

I hope life treats you well,
and as far as I can tell,
we are both right on track —
no need for looking back.

Remember, I always loved you.
I'll always be your friend, too,
because that's what we're supposed to do:
let the love of God, shine through.

He's My Saving Grace

When they call,
He will not answer!
You can serve
only one Master!

God or Satan, see?
Me? I pick God and we
play together, pray together,
and, we'll always stay together.

No matter about the weather,
God, always makes it better.
He keeps me safe in this evil place.

The one none can replace,
He's my saving grace

It's Just Me

Hey Tressa, I came by today,
as I was on my way.
I came to see a boy named Clay,
since I'm his Daddy.

I stopped by to let you know,
Tressa, that I'm headed to bless his little soul.
Then it's off to Mom and Dad's.
Oh, and I am so glad

I don't need a wheelchair
like I did down there.
I have wings now, and I can fly.
I go everywhere.

Just close your eyes,
and you'll see me,
Tressa, I bring healing.

I will take healing
to Mom and Dad too,
but first,
I brought some healing for you.

— Jarvis

The Way I Feel Inside

The way I feel inside,
sometimes I cannot hide.
The hurt you caused
made me put up walls,

and once that begins,
I'm so sorry friend,
it will soon end.
The wheels are starting to spin.

I'm longsuffering, that's true,
but when I am done,
I am *through!*

If you don't believe me,
Just ask my ex;
that's why it ended —
it had nothing to do with sex.

No foundation
from God, above.
Now I know the truth,
and I am free
because of God's love.

Forget those things behind
you. Forget about me.
keep moving forward,
as we all should be.

Why Did You Pick Me?

I asked, "Why did you pick me?"
He said, "You're like a Cedar of Lebanon tree."
My faith is so great.
He is never late.

And God, is my soulmate.
He is simply great.
He doesn't hesitate.

Like I said, He is simply great.
You can count on Him.
He is never late.

"A fallen angel," God said,
"that Devil will soon be dead."
That is what God said.
I thank Him for my daily bread.

By Him, I am led
through the meadows
full of peace instead
of turmoil and grief.
Thank you, God. What a relief.

Tracey, He Is Healing you

I walked in and there was an angel
in the room —
over in the corner
keeping away the gloom.

That Devil, he comes to
steal, kill, and destroy,
but knowing about this angel,
I get great joy.

Because my Father, sent
that angel, to your room,
she'll be there,
morning, night, and noon.

He said He'll never leave you.
He will always be there.
He made you,
and He said He knows life isn't fair,

but when He finally gets there,
it will be worth it all.
Everything He does
is big, not small.

He is the great I AM.
We all know that's true.
Tracey, God said, He is
healing you!

—I LOVE YOU!

She Was Sorry

I ran into the man that cheated
with my Brother's wife.
Well, it doesn't seem like
he's had a very good life.

Then I got a picture, through messenger
of you two,
it had me missing both of you.

Sherry, you were his first true love,
and you're together again.
God, forgave you
in the end.
Together again, they will always be —
Jarvis and Sherry had the Victory!

She was sorry,
and I was her friend.
She told me she was sorry
over and over again.

I felt so bad
for her suffering;
I knew she was in pain.
I prayed — through that whole thing.

I loved her a lot,
and I know Jarvis did too.
Betty Shaw, they're in Heaven,
waiting for you.

Jarvis Loved Sherry

Jarvis loved Sherry Shaw,
and Sherry loved him.
And yes, dear friends,
they are together again.

He went to Heaven,
and so did she.
They were both forty-five
when they left for Heaven,
and now they're both happy as can be.

They made it home.
They are together again.
No more pain;
that was the end.

A new beginning—
They are both healed.
Father God in Heaven
wiped away all of their tears.

Now they are happy,
and forever they will be
home with the Father,
and that is simply Victory.

Jarvis Sent the Snowflakes

The snowflakes are tears,
all different, don't you know.
Each one different,
they land and make snow.

Frozen in time,
great memories,
I wouldn't take nothing
for any of these.

You must be jumping on a snow cloud today,
and now that snow is coming our way.

A sign from my brother
to me, Tress, and Troy
to know his Spirit comes
and then moves on.

He's busy, traveling in the spirit,
can't you see?
He sent the snow
for me and my family.

Curtis Came to Say He's Sorry

You got into my car three times
with our song playing, blowing my mind.
I knew that it was fine in the spirit,
since you came by.

"It's Hard for Me to Say I'm Sorry" came on.
It used to be one of our favorite songs,
back in the day, don't you know.

Well, it was *my* favorite song, anyway.
I was hurt—most every day.
It doesn't matter anymore,
and now I know what it was all for,

and why he had to go:
steppingstones,
lessons in life.
I will always be glad
I was your first and only wife.

Now, it's time to get on with life,
forget all I sacrificed,
let go of the past,
think of my future.
And that is that.

Hey There, Donnie

Hey there, Donnie.
I saw you were sick.
I came to see about you quick.

I'm a spirit now,
and I'm watching over you.
A spiritual being—
believe me, it's true.

I'll always be near you;
this I want you to know.
I will be with you
wherever you go.

Shut your eyes.
Think about me,
and my face
you will see.

I didn't want to leave you.
I love you deep down in my soul.
I didn't want to leave you.
I'm sorry I had to go.

Remember, if you're feeling a little blue,
shut your eyes,
and I will come to you.

I will always be there,
even though you can't see me.
It's me in spirit,
and I will never leave.

— Miss Barbara

A Broken Angel

She is a broken angel.
I know a few,
and their wings,
well, they're a little broken too.

That's okay;
they'll mend in time —
kind of like a song
to mend this broken mind.

I look for a reason not to at all.
When you are broken,
even an Angel can fall.

That is when
we get down on bended knees
and say, "Thank you, Father,
and Father, please…"

He will be there
to make it better every single day,
and if their wings are broken,
then an angel goes away.

She'll be back by, you'll see.
When it is all said and done,
that broken angel was me.

My Four Babies

My four little babies
are my inheritance, you see.
I thank God every day
for all he has given me.

They are little angels,
sent from above.
All they want from anyone
is to be loved.

What some don't know
is this:
God is love.

If they could see,
then they would know
and be happy as can be.

My Father is so wonderful,
we will praise His Holy Name.
When we stand before our Father,
there will be no one for us to blame.

So, I must do it right,
and worship my Father
in spirit and in truth.

I love a church that doesn't care
to praise and worship,
until they raise the roof,

I get excited when I think
about what God has done for me.
But most of all,
I thank him for his Son
and what He did at Calvary.

CPSIA information can be obtained
at www.ICGtesting.com
Printed in the USA
BVHW071446160919
558546BV00007B/864/P

9 781644 381243